SKUNK VS. RACCOON

BY KIERAN DOWNS

TORQUE™

BELLWETHER MEDIA • MINNEAPOLIS, MN

Torque brims with excitement
perfect for thrill-seekers of all kinds.
Discover daring survival skills, explore
uncharted worlds, and marvel at mighty
engines and extreme sports. In *Torque* books,
anything can happen. Are you ready?

This edition first published in 2023 by Bellwether Media, Inc.

Library of Congress Cataloging-in-Publication Data

Names: Downs, Kieran, author.
Title: Skunk vs. raccoon / by Kieran Downs.
Other titles: Skunk versus raccoon
Description: Minneapolis, MN : Bellwether Media, 2023. | Series: Torque: animal battles | Includes bibliographical references and index. | Audience: Ages 7-12 | Audience: Grades 4-6 | Summary: "Amazing photography accompanies engaging information about skunks and raccoons. The combination of high-interest subject matter and light text is intended for students in grades 3 through 7"– Provided by publisher.
Identifiers: LCCN 2022001060 (print) | LCCN 2022001061 (ebook) | ISBN 9781644877623 (library binding) | ISBN 9781648348785 (paperback) | ISBN 9781648348082 (ebook)
Subjects: LCSH: Skunks–Juvenile literature. | Raccoon–Juvenile literature.
Classification: LCC QL737.C248 D69 2023 (print) | LCC QL737.C248 (ebook) | DDC 599.76/8–dc23/eng/20220112
LC record available at https://lccn.loc.gov/2022001060
LC ebook record available at https://lccn.loc.gov/2022001061

Editor: Rebecca Sabelko   Designer: Josh Brink

Printed in the United States of America, North Mankato, MN.

TABLE OF CONTENTS

THE COMPETITORS

Under the cover of night, many animals hunt for food. The darkness helps them avoid **predators**. But they must always be ready. Skunks are known for their powerful stink. Most enemies will run before fighting them.

Raccoons use their senses to find their way in the dark. They also know how to scare away enemies. Who would win in a nighttime battle between these two animals?

STRIPED SKUNK PROFILE

```
0          12 INCHES          24 INCHES
```

LENGTH
UP TO 19 INCHES
(48 CENTIMETERS)

WEIGHT
UP TO 14 POUNDS
(6.4 KILOGRAMS)

HABITATS

GRASSLANDS   DESERTS   CITIES   FORESTS

STRIPED SKUNK RANGE

☐ RANGE

There are 11 different **species** of skunks. They are mostly found in the western half of the world. These **mammals** have black and white fur.

Skunks are **omnivores**. They eat many kinds of **insects**. They also eat small mammals and some plants. These **nocturnal** animals stay in hollow trees or **burrow** into the ground during the day.

Raccoons are also nocturnal mammals. They can be found in parts of North America, South America, Europe, and Asia. They make their homes in many different **habitats**.

Raccoons have gray or brown fur. Dark markings on their faces make a mask around their eyes. They have striped, **bushy** tails. Raccoons are omnivores that eat fruits, seeds, and **rodents**.

FISHING FOR FOOD

Raccoons are strong swimmers. They use this skill to catch fish, frogs, and crayfish to eat.

NORTHERN RACCOON PROFILE

0   12 INCHES   24 INCHES   36 INCHES   48 INCHES

LENGTH
UP TO 37.5 INCHES
(95 CENTIMETERS)

WEIGHT
UP TO 23 POUNDS
(10.4 KILOGRAMS)

HABITATS

FORESTS   MARSHES   PRAIRIES   CITIES

NORTHERN RACCOON RANGE

◼ RANGE

SECRET WEAPONS

Skunks have five long, sharp claws on each paw. They use these to dig holes to look for food. They also use them to attack enemies.

Raccoons use their strong senses to find food in the dark. Their eyes **reflect** extra light. This helps them see close objects more clearly. Their excellent hearing helps them find **prey**.

REFLECTING EYES

SECRET WEAPONS

LONG, SHARP CLAWS

WARNING COLORS

STINKY SPRAY

Skunks have bright white stripes or spots. These patterns stand out from their black fur. The colors warn other animals to stay away.

SECRET WEAPONS

RACCOON

STRONG SENSES

SENSITIVE PAWS

SPEED

SENSITIVE PAWS

Raccoons' paws are even more sensitive when they are wet. This is why raccoons often put their food in water.

Raccoons have highly **sensitive** paws. This helps them know what they are holding in the dark. Their paws are also **adapted** to grab objects. Some raccoons can open jars and untie knots!

SKUNK SPRAY DISTANCE

MORE THAN 10 FEET (3 METERS)

0   4 FEET   8 FEET   12 FEET

Skunks have special **glands** under their tails. These allow the skunks to spray a stinky scent. The spray can travel more than 10 feet (3 meters)!

15 MILES (24 KILOMETERS) PER HOUR

RACCOON

28 MILES (45 KILOMETERS) PER HOUR

HUMAN

Raccoons can run at speeds of up to 15 miles (24 kilometers) per hour! This allows raccoons to escape predators. They are also skilled climbers.

ATTACK MOVES

Skunks hiss at their enemies before a fight.
They stamp their front feet and raise their tails.
They charge forward to try to scare enemies away.

Raccoons also try to scare off enemies before fighting. They make themselves look bigger. Their fur stands up. They round their backs and raise their tails.

A skunk's spray can be smelled from up to 1.5 miles (2.4 kilometers) away.

When predators do not back down, skunks use their stink. The stinky spray sticks to their enemies. The stink is so strong, most enemies run away.

Raccoons hiss and growl at tough predators. Then they attack! They bite their enemies with their sharp **canine teeth**.

READY, FIGHT!

A raccoon bites into a meal. But a hungry skunk wants a taste. The raccoon's fur stands up as it hisses at the skunk. Raising its tail, the skunk does not back down.

The raccoon jumps forward to bite. The skunk hisses and sprays its stink. The smell is too much for the raccoon. It runs away. The skunk has stolen a meal!

GLOSSARY

adapted—well suited due to changes over a long period of time

burrow—to make a tunnel or hole in the ground to use as an animal's home

bushy—thick and furry

canine teeth—long, pointed teeth that are often the sharpest in the mouth

glands—parts of the body that make a substance

habitats—the homes or areas where animals prefer to live

insects—small animals with six legs and hard outer bodies; an insect's body is divided into three parts.

mammals—warm-blooded animals that have backbones and feed their young milk

nocturnal—active at night

omnivores—animals that eat both plants and animals

predators—animals that hunt other animals for food

prey—animals that are hunted by other animals for food

reflect—to send back light

rodents—small animals that gnaw on their food; mice, rats, and squirrels are all rodents.

sensitive—able to notice the parts of things

species—kinds of animals

TO LEARN MORE

AT THE LIBRARY

Downs, Kieran. *Wolverine vs. Honey Badger*. Minneapolis, Minn.: Bellwether Media, 2021.

Felix, Rebecca. *Raccoons Unite*. Minneapolis, Minn.: Lerner Publications, 2021.

Pringle, Laurence. *The Secret Life of the Skunk*. Honesdale, Pa.: Boyds Mills Press, 2019.

ON THE WEB

FACTSURFER

Factsurfer.com gives you a safe, fun way to find more information.

1. Go to www.factsurfer.com

2. Enter "skunk vs. raccoon" into the search box and click Q.

3. Select your book cover to see a list of related content.

INDEX